Wombats

Victoria Blakemore

For Aunt Christy, with love

Table of Contents

What Are Wombats?

Wombats are a special kind of mammal called a marsupial. This means that the females have a pouch on their stomach.

There are three kinds of wombats. They differ in where they live and whether they have hair on their nose.

The common wombat is also called the bare-nosed wombat because it doesn't have hair on its nose.

3

Size

Wombats are usually between two and three feet long. They can grow to be nearly four feet long.

Hairy-nosed wombats are the smaller wombats. They usually weigh between forty and seventy pounds.

Bare-nosed wombats are larger.

They can weigh up to ninety

pounds.

Physical Characteristics

Wombats are very low to the ground. Their size helps them to move quickly when needed.

They have very thick, tough skin on their bottom. The skin is tough enough to withstand a bite from a predator, so they often use it to block the entrance to their burrow.

Wombats have long claws.

They use them to quickly dig

burrows into the dirt.

Habitat

Wombats are found in forests, grasslands, and mountains. It is often very hot during the day and cold at night where wombats live.

They like areas with lots of plants for **camouflage**. The color of their fur helps them to blend in to the brush.

Range

Wombats are found in parts of

southern and eastern Australia.

They are also found on islands

near the coast of Australia.

Diet

Wombats are **herbivores**, which means that they only eat plants.

Their diet is mainly made up of grass. They have also been known to eat moss, herbs, or mushrooms. When it is very dry, they may also eat roots.

Wombats spend many hours

each day **grazing**. They usually

eat at night when it is cooler.

Wombats have very strong teeth and jaws. This helps them to tear the plants they eat.

Plants can be hard for mammals to **digest**. Wombat stomachs have a special **gland** that helps them break down their food.

Wombats get most of their water from the food they eat. They can go for long periods of time without drinking water.

Communication

Wombats use mainly scent and sound to communicate with each other.

They have a special scent that they rub on trees to mark their **territory**. This lets other wombats know that the area is taken.

Wombats use sounds such as growls, grunts, squeals, hisses, and clicks to communicate.

Movement

Wombats are able to run very quickly when needed. They have been **observed** running at speeds of twenty-five miles per hour.

They can also swim very well, although they are rarely seen in the water.

Their short legs and large size

cause wombats to walk with a

waddle.

Wombat Joeys

Wombats have one baby, which is called a joey. Mother wombats keep their baby in their pouch, which is on their belly.

The pouch keeps the joey close and allows the wombat to protect it.

Joeys stay in their mother's

pouch until they are about five

months old.

Wombat Life

Wombats are usually **solitary** animals. However, they can also live in groups called mobs or colonies. They are **nocturnal**, which means they are most active at night.

In the wild, wombats often live between five and eight years.

Wombats are usually very shy and prefer to stay hidden when humans are near. They may become **aggressive** and try to bite if you get too near.

Wombat Burrows

Wombats spend a lot of time resting in burrows. They use their long claws to dig a burrow into the dirt or brush.

Burrows can have many tunnels and **chambers**. They can be used by one wombat or by a mob.

Wombats spend much of the day in their burrow. It helps to keep them cool when it is hot.

Giant Wombats

Giant wombats, or diprotodons, were the largest marsupials. They lived thousands of years ago. They could be ten feet long and weigh 3,000 pounds.

Researchers are not sure why giant wombats went **extinct**. It could have been due to hunting and habitat loss.

Researchers learn about giant

wombats by studying fossilized

bones.

Population

The common wombat and southern hairy-nosed wombat are not currently **endangered.** In some areas, their populations are **declining.**

Wombats face threats such as habitat loss, disease, being hit by cars, and being hunted as **pests.**

The northern hairy-nosed wombat is **critically endangered**. There are thought to be less than 120 left in the wild.

Helping Wombats

National parks like the Epping Forest National Park provide wombats with safe habitats.

Many wombats are killed each year when they try to cross roads in their habitats. Special signs are put along roads to warn drivers to watch out for wombats.

WOMBATS
NEXT
10 km

There are special groups that help wombats that are sick or hurt. They take care of them and release them into the wild when they are well.

Some groups focus on education. They help people protect their land from wombats to help reduce **conflict**.

Glossary

Aggressive: likely to attack

Camouflage: using color to blend in to the surroundings

Chambers: rooms or compartments

Conflict: fight or strong disagreement

Critically Endangered: nearly extinct

Declining: getting smaller

Digest: break down food

Endangered: at risk of becoming extinct

Extinct: when there are no more of an animal left in the wild

Gland: part of the body that makes fluids and releases them into other parts of the body

Grazing: eating grass

Herbivore: an animal that eats only plants

Nocturnal: animals that are active at night

Observed: seen

Solitary: living alone

Territory: an area of land that an animal claims as its own

About the Author

Victoria Blakemore is a first grade

teacher in Southwest Florida with a

passion for reading.

You can visit her at

www.elementaryexplorers.com

Also in This Series

Gray Wolves	**Sloths**	**Flamingos**	**Camels**	**Koalas**	**Honey Bees**
Pandas	**Pangolins**	**White-Tailed Deer**	**Orcas**	**Giraffes**	**Corn**
Meerkats	**Echidnas**	**Walruses**	**Raccoons**	**Bald Eagles**	**Apples**
Arctic Foxes	**Red Pandas**	**Cassowaries**	**Tigers**	**Ladybugs**	**Moose**
Beluga Whales	**Leopards**	**Elephants**	**Jellyfish**	**Binturongs**	**Lions**
Dolphins	**Reindeer**	**Hammerhead Sharks**	**Hippos**	**Pumpkins**	**Peafowl**

Elementary Explorers

Victoria Blakemore

Also in This Series

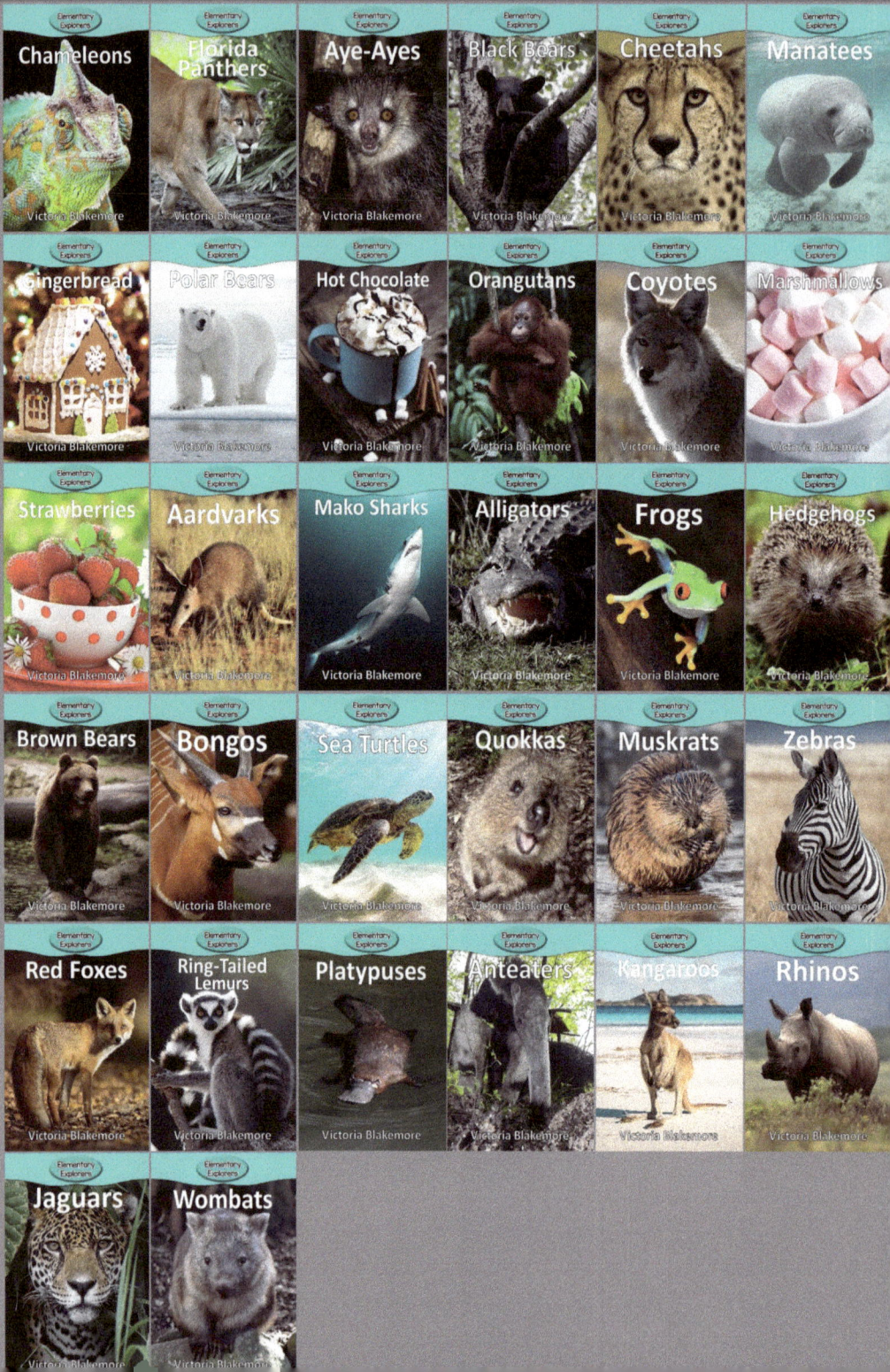

Chameleons	Florida Panthers	Aye-Ayes	Black Bears	Cheetahs	Manatees
Gingerbread	Polar Bears	Hot Chocolate	Orangutans	Coyotes	Marshmallows
Strawberries	Aardvarks	Mako Sharks	Alligators	Frogs	Hedgehogs
Brown Bears	Bongos	Sea Turtles	Quokkas	Muskrats	Zebras
Red Foxes	Ring-Tailed Lemurs	Platypuses	Anteaters	Kangaroos	Rhinos
Jaguars	Wombats				

Victoria Blakemore

www.ingramcontent.com/pod-product-compliance
Lightning Source LLC
Chambersburg PA
CBHW051254020426
42333CB00025B/3210